SO, YOU
THINKING ABOUT
HOME SCHOOLING?

10 Questions to
Ask Yourself Before
Making the Leap

AMANDA GOODCHILD

B&F

Brook & Field Publishing

Dedicated to my husband David who makes our family such a fun place to be.

SO, YOU'RE THINKING ABOUT HOME SCHOOLING? 10 QUESTIONS TO ASK YOURSELF BEFORE MAKING THE LEAP

By Amanda Goodchild

Published by Brook and Field Publishing
www.brookandfieldpublishing.com

Book cover design by nskvsky

With special thanks to Steffanie Moyers for her assistance with editing and proof reading the manuscript.

For permissions contact: info@brookandfieldpublishing.com

ISBN Print Edition 978-1-7397712-3-2

First edition published from the United Kingdom 2022.

Contents

"Would you tell me, please, which way I ought to go from here?'
'That depends a good deal on where you want to get to,' said the Cat.
'I don't much care where -' said Alice.
'Then it doesn't matter which way you go,' said the Cat.

Lewis Caroll, Alice's Adventures in Wonderland

Before we get started

———•• ● •• ———

Dear reader,

I want to begin with a personal note from me to you –
what you can expect from this book, and what you can't.
Firstly, I assume that if you're reading this then you are at
least considering taking your children out of the school
system and educating them yourself. Fair assumption?
Good, then my goal is simply to help you crystalise your
own thinking so that you can make a decision with
confidence, whatever that may be.

I believe powerfully in the value of educational freedom
but I realise that its success heavily depends on us, the
parents (or guardians). There are some families for whom
it simply wouldn't work. That's not their fault; it's not even
a problem; it's just a fact that we're all different and what
may bring joy and delight to one family, can bring pain
and a headache to another.

That said, my intention is not to lead you in a particular
direction, but rather to help you process your own

thoughts and perhaps consider things you may otherwise overlook. I am unashamedly pro-home educating, but if you get to the end of this book and decide it's not right for you, or at least not yet, then as far as I'm concerned, that's great. My job is done.

If you are married or co-parenting, I'd strongly recommend reading through (or at least discussing elements of) this book with your other half. In my experience, it is important for both parents to be on the same page when it comes to the education of their children. As parents we can be fiercely protective of our children, and depending on our perspective and personal experience, we can perceive a disruption to the status quo as a threat. We don't always journey at the same pace either. One parent can reach a new viewpoint much quicker than the other, and I believe it's important to honour that journey in our loved ones and not to force something prematurely. (Just my opinion, take it or leave it!).

Finally, this book is not a "how to home school" manual. You may find that along the way you pick up some ideas, but that's not the goal here.

So, grab a cup of your favourite go-to beverage (mine is coffee or fresh ginger tea), and possibly a journal to record your reflections, and let's get started.

But first, I'll share a little of my own story with you.

Our story

At the time of writing, our children are aged 7, 9, 11 and 13. We took them out of school nearly three years ago. The fact that we are now home educating still catches me by surprise from time to time. It was a totally unexpected detour in what was otherwise going to be a very predictable route that was likely to end with exams and a school graduation. So why was it a surprise? Well for starters – I don't really enjoy spending lots of time with children. (I can handle my own kids but I much prefer the company of adults in general).

Secondly, we loved our children's school and didn't have a single complaint about it. I know a lot of families whose experience with the school system has been dire, but ours was quite the opposite. Thirdly, when I was younger, I said that if I ever had children, I would never home school them (this was based on total ignorance of course!). So, what happened to us and why did we decide to chart a new, and some might say a "riskier" path?

Amanda Goodchild

I believe it was this: a seed was planted – the idea of a different kind of lifestyle and a different sort of education; over time that seed grew into a desire, until the desire to chart a different course became too compelling to ignore. The entire process took about 18 months and grew slowly, but in the end, I was more concerned that I would regret staying in the "safe zone" than I would regret taking a leap into the unknown.

It wasn't an easy decision and my husband and I wrestled with it lot. We asked each other questions and tried to really unearth what was in our hearts. We had to examine our assumptions, our fears and our prejudices. I won't focus on our reasons now, because this book is about you and your reasons, but I just want to say that if you find this choice an agonising one, you are not alone. Eventually though the fog will lift and clarity will come, and hopefully some courage if you need it.

The world is changing. Fast.

We all know the world is changing at a rapid pace, but have you ever asked yourself, why have the technological advancements in the past 20 years altered so many areas of our lives, except for education? Just think about how our society has embraced change. We are all happy to shop online, whether for food, books, make up or clothes. We expect to book holidays or train tickets from our phones, and to consume our favourite entertainment when it suits us. These examples just scratch the surface of how our world is changing.

Stop for a minute and imagine this scenario: you walk into a supermarket and one of the staff members comes along and presents you with a trolley pre-filled with food and items for your weekly shop. Would you say, "Thanks very much," pay the bill and leave with bags full of goods you never picked yourself? Or would you say, "Thanks, but I'd prefer to choose for myself what goes into my trolley," and then proceed to browse the shelves?

Amanda Goodchild

It might sound ridiculous but this is exactly the choice on offer when it comes to education. You can either accept the "tinned education" pre-selected by the store management – also known as the government bureaucracy in charge of education (which may well be an excellent fit for your child and family by the way) – or you can say: "Thanks but no thanks; I'd prefer to choose for myself." Parents who opt to design their own education are finding that the "shelves" are full of high-quality and innovative options like never before.

The explosion in innovation also means many people no-longer work Monday to Friday or 9 - 5. We are used to more flexible working and to having deliveries fit around our diaries. We do online banking, we communicate with friends, family and colleagues online, and even use web-based tools for our hobbies. Artificial Intelligence is still in its infancy, and yet it means that the old rules that we took for granted are no longer given.

Yet despite all this change, the education system as a whole has remained largely static. The curriculum may have changed periodically and teachers may have developed new methods, but the basic concept – that a teacher instructs a classroom of children according to a prescribed curriculum and a pre-determined timetable, culminating in standardised exams, is still very much intact. When the bell goes, the lessons still stop.

I firmly believe that the global pandemic of Covid-19 forced change into the education system sooner than would otherwise have happened, but on the whole, significant change is on the horizon. Unfortunately, there are vast opportunities for education that most school systems simply won't tap into because to do so would require an extraordinary level of vision and courage. Too many people have a vested interest in keeping things the same, or at the very least, there are too few leaders who are bold enough to truly disrupt the culture in order to forge a new one.

There is power in asking questions

Here are a few questions I've been asking myself over the past few years:

- Why do all children in the same classroom have to basically learn the same thing? Here's one example: a typical primary school in the UK has to choose a modern foreign language for its pupils to learn, and then they hire in a teacher. Why can't children (or their parents) choose which language to learn based on their family background and lifestyle, and then enable the children to take that lesson online using a great learning programme? My children are learning Te Reo Maori, Hebrew, Spanish and Latin (albeit in small doses) because these are the languages which are most relevant to us. I totally agree that all children need to reach

13

a basic level of proficiency in literacy and numeracy, but even then, there are a variety of ways to develop that.

- Why can't children who grab a concept quickly (in maths for example), progress through a programme of study faster than their peers, or why are children expected to 'catch up' if they 'fall behind'? Why does our system obsess over children learning at essentially the same pace?

- Why doesn't the government ask itself: "For all the billions we are spending on education, are we getting a good return on investment?" And if it's not good enough, will spending more money really help or do we need more fundamental change?

- Why do so many parents think they are not capable of facilitating a world-class education for their children, given the internet enables them to access world-leading teaching for free or at a very low cost?

- Why do we not place a high value on children being able to pursue their passions at the time of day when they have the most energy?

There are obvious historical reasons why things are the way they are, but just because something started out one way, doesn't mean it has to continue that way.

What questions do you find yourself asking? They reveal what you value and how you see the world so I encourage you to pay close attention.

Now, this is not to beat-up schools. I know first-hand how dedicated most teachers are to the children they teach, but every system needs to challenge its core assumptions on a regular basis to stay relevant. My worry is that when it comes to education, not enough people are asking these sorts of questions.

It's very difficult to imagine just how different the world might be in 10 years, but one thing I do know: the current education system is channelling children down a path that leads to a prescribed set of qualifications which may well become obsolete, or at the very least, be of little value to many of the children who graduate with them. Of course, literacy and numeracy are essential, as is developing a broad knowledge of the world through science, geography and history. A rich exposure to the arts is also vital for well-rounded human development and many schools do this very well, but the majority of teaching taking place in schools is ultimately governed by how it will affect end of year test results and in my opinion, that's the wrong focus.

Amanda Goodchild

In the past couple of weeks my children have enjoyed learning from some truly expert teachers from around the world, in creative writing, piano, drawing and maths. They also learn from world-class "absent" teachers through reading their books and watching their videos. Authors are often highly knowledgeable and passionate about their subject and can be just as good a teacher, and sometimes better, than one standing in the front of a classroom. Engaging with an absent teacher through their written work also requires a high degree of brain power.

Consider also how new platforms are opening up which connect students in Brazil or the UK to universities in the USA or Hong Kong, to name but a few. Game-based learning platforms are popping up all over the place with many incorporating adaptive AI to personalise learning, as are forums and online communities for parents to connect with each other, share ideas, share resources and plan social activities.

Innovation in the education sector has been exploding in recent years, but by and large it's developing *outside* of the traditional school system and filtering in, rather than the other way around. We can be confident that choice and opportunity will only increase, giving our young people even more opportunities to engage with educational experiences beyond a local school.

The world is changing. Fast.

There has never been a better time to reimagine what education can look like, and parents have never been better equipped to do this for their own families if they want to.

Now, onto the questions and hopefully, some thought-provoking conversation.

Question One

What is your dream lifestyle?

— • • ● • • —

I t might seem like an odd place to start but making the decision to educate your children within the school system, or to take responsibility for educating them yourself, is ultimately a lifestyle choice. Making the switch to home schooling is about far more than just what sort of *education* you want your children to have, it's fundamentally about what sort of *lifestyle* you want your family to have.

Many parents love sending their children to school because it means they typically get six hours a day child-free. For parents who need or want to work, this is great. I get it. This was me for several years too. Yes, you may have to endure the school run, and depending on who you are, the chit chat at the school gate can be wonderful or a headache, but let's be honest, childcare is a genuine reason to want to dress your child in that uniform every day and send them off to school. No shame in that.

Perhaps the biggest adjustment to your lifestyle if you choose to home educate, will be having your children around you a lot more. Now this doesn't mean you have to do everything together; on the contrary, you may get a break when they take part in activities such as scouts, sports matches or dance lessons. And even when you are at home, your children won't be hanging around your feet all day, but they will likely be there for breakfast, snack, lunch and dinner, and need a certain amount of quality time with you most days. For some people, that would be a nightmare; for others, spending more quality time with their children when they are not tired and wingy at the end of the day would be welcomed.

For us, the biggest change to our lifestyle has been the freedom it has brought to our diary. On a day-to-day basis it means that we are not governed by the clock. We can choose to have a slow morning if we need to, or to get up bright and early and hit the beach for breakfast if we so desire. We can make the most of the sunshine and start our day with a mountain bike ride if we feel like it. We don't do it every week, but we have the freedom to do so if we want. I've found this freedom really valuable in the winter. Sometimes we can have rain for days on end and when the weather breaks and the sun finally comes out, we are free to make the most of it and get outside.

We also have the freedom to take a day out and visit somewhere new when it suits our family diary. This month my husband had a Wednesday off work so we took a day trip to Stonehenge and Salisbury Cathedral to see the Magna Carta. Spontaneous life experiences and educational enrichment like this happens all the time. In our house we never do our formal learning on someone's birthday, and we take breaks for events that are important to us, but not to the British school system. These are just some of the ways that our lifestyle has changed due to home education, and it was certainly one of the biggest pulls to make the switch in the first place.

What about you? What would your ideal day look like? Would it involve dropping your children off at school and then spending the morning working on your own projects or a paid job, exercising, having coffee with friends or walking the dog? Or would you prefer to have a slower paced morning, perhaps making a healthy cooked breakfast and going for a walk with your children for some fresh air and exercise before sitting down to some reading together?

The school timetable can work really well for families who have an adult working Monday to Friday, 9-5. It is less friendly to those families who don't work a traditional timetable (such as us). Home educating has given us the freedom to plan our time around what is most important to us, rather than feeling like our life is spent running around after other people and what they consider important.

If choosing to home educate impacts on your income, then this will also affect your lifestyle. Finally, I will also say that school brings the potential for meaningful community. I say potential because some parents love their involvement with the school and the friends they make there, while others don't. We certainly did. Choosing to opt-out of school will likely mean opting out of this community, or at least reducing your involvement, which could affect your lifestyle as well. We have kept in touch with the genuine friends we made through school, though from time to time I do miss the daily banter at the school gates. It's not enough to change course mind you – everything is a matter of priorities.

Reflection Point:

Consider your overall lifestyle goals and then think about how educating your children yourself would either help or hinder these. You may find it helpful to write these down.

Question Two

What would you miss most about school?

——— • • ● • • ———

If your children have never been to school then this question will be mostly hypothetical, though you will probably draw from your own experience of school growing up. If we are honest, most of us will have at least one or two things that we would miss, or that we think our children would miss, if they didn't attend school. Try and be honest with yourself about this.

In our household, most of the time we don't miss anything, but occasionally I think that my children would enjoy some of the clubs on offer, or the chance to be in a school play (that said, my children's primary school only did a Nativity play in the junior school which I am not a big fan of, and a production for the school leavers upon graduation, with little opportunities for children in the middle years).

Q 2 - What would you miss most about school?

It's okay to miss something; it doesn't mean that leaving the school system is the wrong choice. Grief or loss is part of making choices. I raise this question because it's important to manage your own expectations before you start out.

Consider also that there is a big difference between missing out on something and actually missing something. Everyone misses out on something, including the rich and famous. Even if my children attended the best school money can buy, they can't try every sport or do everything under the sun. Wealth, privilege, opportunity and the lack thereof will always mean there are things we will simply never get to do. Thankfully, we don't need to do everything or experience everything in planet earth to be happy. Humans can be content with simple lives, and in some ways, the simpler the life, the happier we are.

Missing something is different. That's when we experience the emotions of loss or sadness. This can sometimes even become jealousy and self-pity. Perhaps the more important issue then, is whether you feel your child will *feel* a strong sense of loss about school, and if so, whether the new experiences and opportunities on offer through home schooling will outweigh these.

If your list is very short, that will help give you greater confidence to move forward with home education. If your list is very long, you will likely need some compelling

Amanda Goodchild

reasons to tip the scales in favour of leaving school. Hopefully as you meditate on these things throughout this book, what is really important will rise to the surface and you'll know what's best for your family.

Reflection Point:

Make a note of all the things you think your children would genuinely miss or pine for if they weren't at school, and then do the same for yourself - what would you as the parent miss out on?

Question Three

What sort of education do you want for your children?

———— • • ● • • ————

Are we even allowed to ask that?

Before we get into this one, let's start by stating the obvious: this is a question that our society does not really want parents to ask. It throws up too many challenges for an already stretched education system. Instead, we are encouraged to accept what is offered without complaining too much. (Remember the supermarket trolley?) After all, it's difficult enough for schools to provide a well-rounded education that challenges children academically, nurtures their creativity and keeps social cohesion in the classroom and on the playground, without adding in the pressure to try and please the unique whims and wishes of hundreds of parents. We are expected to just be grateful that we have access to such good education (and childcare) and not demand too much.

Amanda Goodchild

Now, I must say that on one level I agree with this. I am conscious that my children were born into privilege by virtue of their citizenship. On balance, the state school system in the UK provides a high standard of education compared to many other countries in the world – and for free! I know many parents in poorer countries would move heaven and earth to give their children access to the sort of education that we have access to, and often take for granted. Also, I believe that if parents choose to enrol their child in the school system, then it is unfair to expect the school to accommodate all their personal preferences. Schools have to find the best fit for the majority, and within a budget, and sometimes that will mean they make decisions some parents won't agree with. That's their right and parents should save their complaints for genuine concerns.

With those disclaimers out of the way, let's return to the question at hand. What sort of education do you want for your children? I encourage you to ask this because you are lucky enough to live in a time when you don't *have* to accept what's on offer, even if it's really good. If you want something different to the National Curriculum and its limited qualifications, now more than ever, you have the ability to provide an alternative. In previous generations this privilege was limited to the wealthy, but it's more affordable than ever to design the sort of education that your family wants.

Just think about how much has changed in 200 years.

Q 3 - What sort of education do you want for your children?

"When Queen Victoria initially came to the throne schools were for the rich. Most children never went to school and struggled to read or write. Children from rich families were typically taught at home by (a) governess until the age of 10 years old. Wealthy boys from the age of 10 would then go to Public schools such as Rugby. Girls on the other hand continued to be educated at home." (Victorianchildren.org)

In the first half of the 1800s, only the rich went to schools, while the really rich (and royalty) were educated at home by a governess or a tutor. Girls it seems, fared worse than boys.

Have you ever considered that you – yes you! – are very likely capable of providing an education that matches what the young Princess Victoria received from her governess? This doesn't undermine the knowledge and skills of that governess but we've come a very long way since then. Nowadays many parents have university degrees (something completely unheard of in those days), and we have access to the internet with a world of knowledge at our fingertips, expert teachers at our service, and companies like Amazon and eBay ready to post virtually any home learning resource we might want with next day delivery. And let's not forget the growing army of small businesses providing innovative learning solutions to parents around the globe.

Amanda Goodchild

Our access to education need not be restricted by geography either. Take, for instance, Khan Academy, a not-for-profit online learning platform whose mission is to "provide a free, world-class education for anyone, anywhere." Children in India, Haiti, Thailand and Sweden can all access their excellent courses for free, seven days a week. That means your child can too, if they want to.

I say all this to make the simple point that if there was ever a time to ask the question, "what sort of education do you want your children to have?" now is a great time, because chances are, you'll be able to find a way to do it, or at least come close.

What's really important to you in the long-run?

So now I want you to allow yourself to dream a little. Let your imagination wander and see where it leads you.

What sort of education do you really want for your children? Are you satisfied with the National Curriculum? Do you even know what's in it?

Do you want your children to focus on finding their passion at an early age, and be able to devote more time to doing what brings them alive?

How important is it to you for your children to learn based on their interests, as in the Unschooling or Montessori philosophies?

Q 3 - What sort of education do you want for your children?

Do you love the classical educational approach whose goal is a well-ordered mind with the ability to think critically and logically?

Do you like the idea of Unit Studies and being able to really dive deep into a subject and discover it from all angles, making connections – you know – the way things work in the real world?

Perhaps you love the idea of your children leaving school with good grades in your country's chosen qualification, to provide a clear pathway to the university of your choice?

Do you want your children to learn specific languages, or how to start a business?

Perhaps you want your children to be part of a strong school community and all that goes with it E.g., representing the school in sports and competitions, performing end-of-year recitals and taking leadership roles in structures such as school councils. Some adults had an entirely positive experience at school and really want their children to be able to have the opportunity to experience the same as they did (whether they will or not is another matter as our children are seldom just like us).

Do you even dream about world-schooling and travelling with your children to different countries and cultures?

Reflection Point:

I encourage you to make a long list of what you really want your child's education to include, covering as much as you can, and then highlight the top 10.

From there, begin to ask yourself how you might be able to create such a lifestyle/education for your children if you decided to do it yourself. Scope out the possibilities and research what tools are already available to help you. Demystifying your ideas and dreams by adding some tangible plans to them, however loose they may be, can really help to solidify your thinking.

Question Four

What are you most afraid of?

———— • • ● • • ————

F ear. It's a pretty big deal. It governs our choices more than we realise, including education.

My husband recalls that on the first day our children stayed home instead of going back to school, he was pretty anxious. He was worried about what the neighbours might think when they saw our children playing in the garden. He was worried that they weren't following a strict timetable. It's laughable to us now but at the time it *felt* real.

He now says openly:

> "I realised that in the early days I subconsciously felt better when my children were in a school uniform and sitting in a classroom. I felt better just knowing they were in an institution being supervised by proper teachers, regardless of whether they were learning anything. I didn't feel comfortable seeing my son

doing maths in his own clothes. I knew it was completely irrational, but the fear still felt real."

This is just him being honest. I had my own fears, which I will say, have now evaporated entirely.

In my experience, the three most common fears about home education typically manifest in these sorts of questions:

1. Will my child be lonely or grow up to be socially awkward?

2. Will they learn what they need to learn in order to get the qualifications they need in order to get a job or a place at university or college?

3. Will they miss out on really fun things, like being in the school play or being a prefect? (These are totally subjective examples of course – one of my children hated sports days and school plays!)

Some fears are legitimate. They highlight to us that something is dangerous and that we shouldn't just jump head-first without assessing the risk and the severity of the consequences if things go wrong. If you find yourself conflicted, holding both dreams and fears about the idea of home education in tandem, you are not unusual. It is reasonable to be cautious, but it is also reasonable to really examine whether our fears are valid.

Let's examine these particular fears in turn and see whether they hold up to scrutiny.

The fear of having socially awkward kids who become socially weird adults

Jumping back to the previous question, you'll recall that 200 years ago only the rich went to school in the UK; in fact, school attendance was only made mandatory from 1870. As far as the gamut of human history goes, that's pretty recent. Groups of learners gathering around a teacher is an ancient practice and is found in many cultures, but it is not how the majority of the population spent their time. School as we know it now is a fairly new invention, meaning human beings have been doing fine at learning how to read, write, count and create things like art, music or buildings – to talk to each other, strike bargains, enter into trade agreements, start wars, end wars, and fall in love – long before compulsory schooling came along.

So how did humans socialise before school? In their family for starters, and their local geographic community or their tribe. Everything from religious institutions to work and neighbours provided opportunities for people to develop relationships and grow in their ability to get on with different sorts of people. The same opportunities exist for home educated children and young people today, though they will certainly look different around the globe.

Amanda Goodchild

What does it take to become a socially confident adult? Here are my top six but you may have more:

1. A strong family where children are loved unconditionally. 100% this is the most important, but even then, there are some people who rise above the worst of family backgrounds and develop phenomenal resilience, determination and compassion. A strong family will set up most children for a strong adulthood, but nothing is guaranteed in this world.

2. True friends – but we don't need hundreds. Some people only need a couple of good friends to be happy, especially those who are more introverted by nature. School can provide the potential for friends, but not every child finds a BFF at school, and some feel very isolated in the middle of the crowd. Also, just think – do you see your friends every day? I doubt it. As adults, we might see our friends once a week, once a month, or even less. That is the real world of life; it is school which creates an artificial social experience and leaves us feeling that unless our children see their friends every day, they won't have any. It simply isn't true. If you choose to home educate, you may need to be intentional about helping your child make friends, but once they have a couple, for most children, that will be enough.

3. Community – this can come in all sorts of ways such as churches or religious communities, sports teams, clubs such as Brownies or Scouts, doing lessons with other people like horse riding, ballet or belonging to an orchestra. Schools obviously may offer a strong community to belong to, but not every child enjoys this.

4. Opportunities to be a part of a team – being able to work in a team is quite important nowadays, though some adults and children really do prefer working and creating on their own, and that is absolutely fine. Schools can provide children with opportunities to work in teams, but so can home educating parents if they are intentional about it.

5. Knowing our manners and appropriate social etiquette – every culture and society has unspoken rules of engagement, and if you play by the rules, whether it be standing in a queue or saying "please" and "thank you", you're more likely to gain respect and trust. Schools can certainly help train children in this, but they can also foster poor social skills. Why? Because children are spending a huge portion of their time with their peers (who are generally just as immature as they are), rather than with role models (who show us how to behave well in a variety of social settings). School can be very good at teaching people how to survive in the social environment that is school,

but that social environment is not representative of the real world. In the real world, we don't work with people who were all born the same year as us now do we?

6. Social resilience and managing conflict – I believe this is very important, especially for people who aspire to leadership roles. Whether or not school is the best way to develop social resilience depends on the school, and your child. Children can experience bullying, sexual harassment and petty nastiness at school and for some people, it can leave life-long scars and trauma. For others, it can make them stronger. But do you need to go to school to develop this? No. The most powerful tool is an intentional parent. When we model to our children how we personally handle conflict and unpleasant social interactions, we set them an example to follow. When we are vulnerable about our own battles, we can help them process their own social 'wins' and 'fails', and coach them in kindness, courage and how to walk with honour towards our fellow human beings.

Reflection Point:

What else would you add to my list? Ask yourself what character traits or social skills you value as important, and then compare and contrast all the ways that school and home education could develop this in your child.

When considering the above, and your own reflections, do you think these are legitimate fears or really just a fabrication of something else?

The fear of not learning 'enough', or not learning the 'right thing'

The next big fear I want to tackle is the subconscious fear a lot of us have that if we educate our children outside of the school system, they won't learn enough, or they won't learn the right things and consequently, won't succeed. Now some readers may be totally fine in this area and already liberated from the false notion that there is one linear path to success and our children must stay inside the herd to stay on that path; if that's you – all power to you! Feel free to skip ahead to the next section. For the majority of parents though there might be a nagging fear somewhere inside that our children can only succeed within the system. I believe it's a total lie, and when you see the truth of the matter, it can truly set your heart free to educate your children with confidence.

Firstly, let's consider some successful people who had very little formal schooling:

- Thomas Edison – arguably America's most successful inventor – had only three months of schooling. He was taught reading, writing and maths from his mother, and his own curiosity propelled him to learn many things on his own.

- Benjamin Franklin – writer, scientist and leading American statesman – he attended school for two years, and left when he was only 10. He developed his talents through reading, apprenticeships and above all, his own desire to grow.

- Charles Dickens – the celebrated English novelist – left school at the age of 12 and went to work for 10 hours a day.

- Abraham Lincoln – the American President who emancipated millions of African Americans from slavery, was largely self-educated with only sporadic school attendance.

- Leonardo da Vinci – one of the world's artistic and scientific geniuses, received no formal education as he was born illegitimate. He was taught some elementary skills in his father's household, and then became an apprentice. He was, however, extremely observant and curious.

- Caroline Herschel received a very basic education at home (mostly from her father) and went on to make breakthrough discoveries in astronomy and was the first woman in England to hold a government position.

Not everyone is going to make a name for themselves, and for most of us, being happy in life is all we need to be successful, but it's worth remembering that a person's inner drive and curiosity will have a very big impact on their future. Once a person knows how to learn something, there really are no limits. In fact, the straight and narrow curriculum offered in many schools can limit children's potential more than we realise.

Getting back to the fear in question, one of the reasons why it can be so paralysing is because our society mistakenly thinks that unless a child achieves certain grades at school, they will never be able to attend their chosen university, which in turn, will prevent them from pursuing their chosen career.

Firstly, since when did universities have a monopoly on knowledge and wisdom, as if people can't learn, discover or create anything meaningful outside of these institutions? Secondly, I and many others firmly believe that the university system as we know it is in the early stages of a radical deconstruction. Many universities simply won't exist in the coming years, while new ones will spring up offering a much broader range of learning opportunities and qualifications. The platform technology revolution is upending the old rules.

Consider Coursera.org, which enables students from anywhere in the world to enrol in accredited learning programmes, from certificates to fully fledged degrees, with universities and education providers globally. The interconnectedness of our world means my children don't feel restricted to the UK National Curriculum, because they may not even want to attend a UK university. They may start a degree programme with a university in America, or Hong Kong, and they may start it earlier than their peers and all from their laptop at home. Or, they may study a non-university programme; one of my daughters is quite interested in learning with the Interior Design Institute which offers its courses online.

Institutions such as the Open University in the UK enable anyone to access higher education without the same rigid entry requirements found in traditional universities. In the 'old world' I grew up in, places at a university were limited based on the physical size of the campus and the seats in the lecture halls. This meant there was competition for places. Now, with lectures and tutorials all available online, and hybrid options for distance and in-person learning, those restrictions become obsolete. More and more universities are going global and competing for students, rather than students competing for places. Flexibility in learning timeframes is increasing, and costs are coming down. All that to say, previous generations may have had more cause for worry about diverting from the formal route to higher education, but it is not the case for today's young people.

Reflection Point:

Do you perceive that the educational landscape is changing and what do you think about it?

FOMO

Everyone has to face the dreaded Fear of Missing Out (FOMO) at some point in their life, and home educating parents can feel this on their children's behalf, worrying about all the things they might love about school and will miss out on if they don't go. This of course totally depends on the child in question as they all enjoy different things.

I do believe for some children, the experiences provided by school are genuinely positive and for them, FOMO is not just a fear, it's a reality. They would hate to miss out on the chance to represent the school team, banter in the lunch room or perform in front of an assembly. We asked our children what they would miss most about school and then thought hard about how we could create alternative experiences for them that would meet that need, just in a different way.

Just last night I took my older children and two of their friends to London to see a live performance by the Royal Shakespeare Company. It was a Wednesday and we got home at midnight. Thankfully, I could let them sleep in the next day as we weren't at the mercy of the school bell. Would that experience have happened if they weren't home educated? In our case, probably not. Was it valuable? Absolutely!

Reflection Point:

Try writing down all the things that your child might miss out on if they *don't* attend school. Then ask yourself, what experiences or opportunities might they miss out on if they *do* attend school? Are you worried about missing out on *those*?

Take time to reflect on your fears and don't brush them under the carpet. If they are valid, take stock, but if they are not, then stare them down until they no longer frighten you.

Reflection Point:

- Do you know what your biggest fears are? If so, write them down and then look at each one objectively. What is it based on?

- What can you do to prevent the 'problem' you're afraid of from happening?

- Are there steps you could take to reduce the risk or likelihood of those fears materialising?

Question Five

What are you willing to compromise on?

————•●●●●•———

In this world we will all have to compromise on something (even the super-rich). When it comes to education, this is true whether you send your children to school or home school them.

If your children go to school you will have to compromise some of your freedom, and by virtue of the fact your children will learn according to the school's curriculum and testing process, you may have to compromise on *what* your children are learning and *how*. Now if freedom over your time is not that important to you then this won't feel like much of a compromise. Equally, if you love the curriculum and don't really have any desire for your children to learn differently, then being taught the school's way won't feel like a compromise. If, however, you really want your children to be able to learn differently, and to spend their time on their passions or have more experiences outside of the classroom, then school could feel like a compromise.

For the majority of parents, their child's safety and wellbeing is something they won't compromise on. If attending school is sending their child into depression, self-harm, illness or extreme anxiety, then they may well be willing to put everything else aside and prioritise their child's physical and emotional health.

Sometimes when our red lines are crossed in this way, the choice becomes very easy. Many parents have decided that their only option was to remove their child from school or risk the tragedy of a suicide or long-term damage. These are extreme cases though and for the majority of parents it's a case of balancing up competing priorities and working out what they can live without and what they can't.

Reflection Point:

I encourage you to make another list. What are you willing to compromise on and what are you not? If you are able, try and rank them in order of priorities.

Question Six

How comfortable are you with risk?

———— • ● ● ● • ————

When the people in our life first heard that we had chosen to home educate, I was surprised at how often they would say things like: "Wow, you're brave."

Bravery. It implies a willingness to take a risk.

It surprised me because I didn't feel particularly brave; perhaps because I had examined the idea and the very root concept of education so thoroughly, I could see quite clearly that both routes had risks. Yes, home education was riskier on the surface, but then for us, following the predictable path also had risks.

So how comfortable are you with risk? If you find taking risks difficult, you may feel that you need all your questions answered in advance, or to know where your children want to go and how they are going to get there.

This is not a good thing or a bad thing, just something to be self-aware about because people with a low tolerance for risk can end up experiencing higher levels of anxiety. Risk, resilience and versatility are often correlated – at least in my experience.

Our risk appetite can also be a reflection of how much we trust ourselves to make good out of a bad situation, or to pick ourselves up and be successful if it all goes wrong. So another way to think about this question is, do you trust yourself (and your children) to be okay if you start out and then realise it isn't working? Would you feel like you had to prove to yourself that you could make it work at all costs? Or would you be able to honestly assess the situation and say, "We tried, it didn't work, we're still okay. It's time for Plan B."

If you would be okay with failing (and only you can judge what that might look like), then you will likely be more able to take the risk with confidence.

If you are naturally more risk-averse, you might just need to do more research and eliminate the mystery before starting out.

Reflection Point:

Consider these questions and discuss with yourself and/or your partner:

- What feels most 'risky' to me about the idea of home educating?

- What are the risks associated with staying in the school system?

- What can we do to mitigate the risks of both options?

- Would it feel unbearable if the taking the risk to home school turned out in 'failure' or would we be okay?

Question Seven

What about home educating most excites you?

---•·•●•·•---

I believe it's very important to ask yourself, what is it about home educating that gets you most excited? Is it the idea that your children will have the opportunity to learn differently, and in a way that is more aligned with your values? Is it the possibility of how you might be able to spend your time, and the memories you will be able to create as a result? Are you most excited about your children becoming more independent and free thinkers, or simply having their mental health on track after a season of trauma from school?

Knowing your core reasons for wanting to educate your children yourself is really helpful on the days when things don't feel like they are going to plan, like when your children fight and argue or if nothing gets done. It's also important as you move through the journey to remain anchored to what excites you as the push and pull of new trends, curricula, resources and opportunities will vie for your attention and it can be all too easy to drift from one thing to another without ever really DOING the things you REALLY want to do.

In our family, a big pull towards home educating was the ability to travel mid-week when my husband has more flexibility over his work. We wanted to be able to get away in our caravan more often, or just spend a day visiting a cultural heritage site here in the UK. Every month I make sure we schedule an outing, day trip or experience, to make the dreams we had the beginning a reality.

I was also excited about what interests might emerge in my children if they had more time to explore the world, and I was excited about the idea of being able to teach them more about the history, language and culture of New Zealand where I came from, as this is part of their heritage, and not something that the British school system would ever do.

Excitement is like oxygen and fuel for a fire. Without it, the spark will die. With it, a whole forest can light up.

Reflection Point:

Make your own list of all the things that excite you about the prospect of home schooling – write down as many things as you like – anything at all that gets you excited. This process alone can help you determine whether you want to give it a try.

Question Eight

What pressures might home educating create?

———— • • ● • • ———

If your children are already in school then you will probably be aware that the school involvement can create all sorts of pressures – not being late, remembering homework, having a clean uniform, invites to birthday parties, school dinner money – and the rest. As children progress through to adolescence then you can add in the pressures of having a mobile phone, exposure to inappropriate content such as pornography, and of course – exams.

What about home education? It will create its own pressures and it's not always possible to predict what they might be. They will also be different for each family. Nevertheless, here are a few things that could *potentially* create pressure:

Q 8 - What pressures might home educating create?

1. Sibling tension from children spending more time with their brothers and sisters.

2. Reduced income if one parent needs to stop working or reduce their work output.

3. Relational pressure from family or friends who disapprove of your decision.

4. Dealing with the Local Authority or government agencies. (Not everyone does have contact with their LA and people's experience varies around the country and across countries).

5. Emotional strain if children are lonely or take time to make new friends.

6. Rejection from school friends if they don't want to associate with you/your child any more.

7. Financial pressure if you feel the need to spend a lot on resources or lessons.

8. Marital stress if your other half doesn't support you or agree with your approach.

9. Friction between you and your child if they refuse to cooperate.

10. If a child refuses to learn anything or shows no interest in the world.

11. Childcare if you need/want to work part time or need respite for self-care.

12. A small home or living remotely with limited access to libraries, galleries, sports facilities etc.

In our house, the biggest source of pressure is really item one, and that's because I've got four children of different ages who know how to wind each other up! Sometimes they learn together beautifully and other times they distract each other or are downright annoying. My strategy to reduce the pressure is always to separate them out into different physical spaces. Initially, I tried to do quite a lot of family group learning but not anymore. There were just too many opportunities for fights which created a lot of stress for me. It wasn't fun. Currently we only do a few things together as a whole group (nature study, recitation and history), but everything else they do on their own or in pairs. I am grateful that we've had very little pressure from the other items on that list but I'm sure that for some families, they could present a challenge.

When a pressure point does arise, it's important to assess the root cause and then be willing to adapt and change. There will nearly always be an alternative waiting to be discovered so it doesn't mean you need to throw in the towel.

Sometimes we simply put unhealthy levels of pressure on ourselves and the only way to relieve that is to keep our self-talk in check, resist the temptation to compare ourselves or our children with others, take a break, examine what's under the surface in our hearts, and sometimes just re-charge with a bath and an early night to bed.

Reflection Point:

- Looking at the list above, and any other ideas of your own, what do you think might be the top three stress points or pressure drivers for your family if you pursued home schooling?

- Can you think of ways you could reduce that pressure?

- What aspects of school involvement would create the most pressure for you?

Question Nine

What are your options if home schooling 'fails'?

━━━━ • ● ● • ━━━━

No one plans to fail, but if you know what your options are if things go wrong, that will reduce the riskiness of your decision, which will in turn increase your confidence.

For different families, failure can look very different. What would it look like to you? – that's is the real question.

It's important to remember that sometimes we can feel like a failure when we're actually not. There are days, weeks, even months when it's just hard and that's normal. Remember too that some schools are *certified failures* and every teacher has 'bad days' when they get home and question whether they ever want to set foot in a classroom again! Finding home educating hard doesn't automatically mean your child is better off in school; it may just be a sign that you need to change something about your approach.

If things do reach a crisis point, sitting down with your child and involving them in any decisions about their education and giving them more say over what they do and how they do it can produce immediate results. Many would already be doing this, but if not, it's a good place to start.

Next, do you know where to find support? Do you know anyone you can personally meet up with for encouragement or to chat things over with? Is there any friendly person on Instagram, Facebook or YouTube who might be willing to talk to you over Zoom or meet for a coffee? New online networks and groups are popping up around the world which help connect parents in the same boat and give them lots of support.

Sometimes we need to create a short-term solution while we work out a longer-term one. If you decide to re-enrol them in a school, an important question to know from the outset is how quickly can you reasonably expect to get a place at a school you would be happy with?

In the meantime, or if you are forced to wait, what could you do differently to reduce the root of the problem or crisis? Are you able to find different resources? Could you prioritise your child's emotional well-being and get them booked into some lessons or classes doing their favourite activity?

It would be worth finding out, if your preferred school is full, what are the other options where you live, and what is the likelihood of getting into one of them? If you cannot get a space in your preferred school, are you happy enough with the other options or is it not worth risking a safe spot in your preferred school?

If you are finding home schooling really isn't working then rest assured, the relevant team at your local authority will likely be very keen to help you get a suitable school place for your child. Things can be more complicated if your child is not well-served by the mainstream school system and needs a specialist school. I am no expert here and I know that many families with additional needs or learning differences find getting a suitable school place for their child a real challenge.

Another solution can be flexi-schooling, where the child spends an agreed amount of time at school, and the rest of their week learning at home. The success of this approach probably comes down to the class teacher, the school leadership and the parents in question, and all the parties' willingness to trust one another and work in a spirit of partnership. I know of many parents who are requesting a flexi-schooling arrangement with their child's school and it is working well.

The core of the issue is, if things fall apart (and if they do then chances are you could feel pretty bad about it) what are your options and how would you go about moving forward? Because seeing a way forward is vital.

Reflection Point:

- What do you think 'failure' in home education would look like for your family?

- What is a possible strategy if 'all else fails'?

- What are your options for local schools, or online schools/distance learning? Could you fund those?

- Where could you get support if you felt you were in an emergency?

Question Ten

How does your close family feel about the idea?

---·•●•·---

The final question I want you to ask is by no means the least important. In my opinion, it can be make or break. There can be lots of people impacted by the decision to educate at home, and if you choose to begin the journey, having all your team on board can be a game changer.

Firstly, if you are married or co-parenting with your partner, then their views are just as important as yours. It's so important to be in sync with each other over *why* you are choosing to home educate (or not if that is the best outcome) and what your *expectations* are. It is worth taking longer over your decision but move forward in agreement, than to make a hasty move without a solid foundation of unity. Why? Because your decision will be tested at some point.

Q 10 - How does your close family feel about the idea?

It might be tested if your child says something about being lonely. It might be tested if you get a nasty comment from a friend or even a total stranger (I never have and I do think it's rare, but it can happen!). Your decision might be tested when your friends tell you about all the great things their children are doing in school, or on a day when your children are arguing non-stop and the tension in your home is tangible, because let's be honest, siblings fight!

When your decision is tested, you need to remember your *Why*. You need to go back to what excites you about this path, and you'll need to remind each other of all the good things you've gained. What you won't want in those moments is an argument with your husband (or wife or partner) and an "I told you so" look or comment. It's so much better if you can face those moments *together*.

What can you do if your partner is not on board? First of all, respect where they are at. Listen to their concerns. Request you set aside time to intentionally talk through some of the issues raised in this book. Get to know each other's heart and recognise that they are motivated by love just as you are. Perhaps do some more research to help address specific concerns or questions. Remember that we all have a different risk appetite so it may simply be that your spouse/co-parent needs more information and concrete plans.

Depending on your situation, it could also be helpful to talk to grandparents, especially if you might call on them for childcare at any point. Also, knowing where they stand means you are well prepared and won't be taken by surprise further down the track.

What if they express concern? Well, that is just an opportunity for you to share your enthusiasm, your dreams and your deep *Why*. I personally believe that much scepticism is simply based on the natural fear many of us have of the unknown. As you begin to share your motivations and they have a chance to see what home education looks like in practice, you may well find their scepticism is replaced with support. Our families were supportive from the outset and that support has grown over time as they see the fruit of our decision. Also, over the past three years we've enjoyed a high degree of support from all sorts of people in the community who have been very eager and willing to support us and our children's learning in different ways.

If you and your partner have similar priorities for your lifestyle, your children's education and how you plan to face the unknowns, then that's wonderful. Chances are you'll both reach the same decision. Walking in unity is the ideal way to begin the journey of educational freedom.

What about your children?

It might sound obvious but your children will no doubt have some strong opinions about their own education and the more you are all in agreement, the smoother life can be. I think it is important to at the very least listen to our children and their wishes, even if we as parents decide to take a different course.

How you speak to them about it will probably depend on their age and maturity, as well as their personality and what you already know about their like or dislike of school. Younger children find it much harder to imagine what school is really like if they've never been; they are also rather adaptable and tend to go with the flow.

We decided to speak to our two older children about the idea of home schooling before making a decision as it was important to know how they felt about the concept, but we didn't talk to our younger children until much later. You will need to decide for yourself what is best for your family, but making the effort to empathise with our children and listen to their hopes and concerns is a powerful way to express our love for them, and in my opinion, love is the best environment for learning so it's good to start on the right footing.

Reflection Point:

- How does your spouse/partner or closest family feel about the idea of home schooling?

- How do you think your children feel or might feel?

- Out of ten, how would you rate the overall level of unity?

Navigating your next step

If after much research, consideration and discussion, you do decide to remove your children from the school system, you will need to find out what the rules are in your country or state, and this can be discovered through a simple online search. It is important to understand what your legal rights and obligations are so that you can move forward confidently.

You may also want to spend some time researching and learning about different educational philosophies and methods before making a decision. There are some excellent videos on YouTube that contrast and compare different pedagogical styles. Some of the most popular are Unschooling, Unit Studies, Classical Education (not to be confused with what is taught in schools today), Charlotte Mason (my personal favourite), Montessori, Warldorf, Steiner and more. Many people find that they have a natural bent towards one approach but end up being somewhat eclectic in practice. Spending time researching these methods is likely to help you crystalise what sort of education you want your children to have, as well as spark some creative ideas of your own.

It could also be worth joining some groups on platforms such as Facebook and have a look through their message history to see what sort of events and activities are being organised in your local area, and the kind of support that parents provide. You can even reach out and ask if anyone local would be willing to meet with you at a local park and talk things over. I've also enjoyed hearing from children themselves on YouTube about their experience of life learning outside the school system.

So, there we have it – 10 questions to ask yourself to help you make a confident choice about whether home educating is right for you. I encourage you to take your time, be honest with yourself and your family and do due diligence. *Remember that this decision does not have to be permanent.* It might end up being a season in your life for a given period of time that simply adds a different dimension to your family's history. Or, you may decide that school really is the best route for your family, in which case, you can weather the inevitable 'storms' knowing that it is still the best option for you.

Whatever you choose, do it with courage. Do it with confidence. Do it with joy. And if you need to change your mind later on, make that choice too. Life really is the sum of all our little choices, and the big ones too.

"In the end that was the choice you made, and it doesn't matter how hard it was to make it. It matters that you did."

Cassandra Clare, City of Glass

About the Author

Amanda Goodchild is currently home educating her four children, which typically involves reading lots of wonderful books, getting up close with nature and exploring the big wide world. Prior to this she worked in marketing with a focus on public relations and spent more than 8 years in different governance roles within the Early Years and Primary School system in the UK.

Amanda also enjoys writing. Her first book, *Lilia and the Giant Bumblebee,* is an original children's picture book, available on Amazon worldwide.

She has also created a unique copywork curriculum for home educators around the world. You can find out more at www.copyworkcave.com

Amanda is a total fan of mountain biking, Vivaldi, Shakespeare and baking Challah bread. Occasionally she finds time to vlog on YouTube as "Home school Hack."

Connect with her on Instagram @homeschoolhack.

"Please can I ask a small favour? If you've found this book helpful at all, please can you take two minutes to write a short review of the book on Amazon? I'd be so grateful. Thank you!" - Amanda